Sugar Free Baking

by

NICOLE BEARDSLEY

THE HAPPY ·PARENT· PROJECT

Whole foods. Natural healing. Happy thoughts.

Copyright
Text copyright © Nicole Beardsley 2013
Photography copyright © Lauren Glucina

All rights reserved. No part of this book may be reproduced or transmitted by any person or entity in any form or by any means without prior permission from the author.

My Purpose

When I asked myself the question "What is my purpose?' the answer, without conscious thinking was "to heal others". The recipes in this book were created by me at a time that my daughter required great healing, and they worked. I give you these recipes in the hope that you will use them to heal your own family.

NICOLE BEARDSLEY

Whole foods. Natural healing. Happy thoughts.

THE HAPPY PARENT PROJECT

"Knowing what fussy creatures kids can be, Nicole as an experienced Mum has created the perfect healthy baking solutions with 'yum' factor!"

- Samantha Spunner, founder of Sinchies Food Pouches

"Sugar Free Baking for busy families fills a gap that other sugar free baking recipe books miss - the recipes are simple and affordable. Not only has each recipe been designed to have amazing flavour for our children's sometimes fickle tastebuds, they have also each been designed to be visually enticing to little eyes"

- Alice Nicholls, Health & Wellness Coach & Wellness Business Mentor, The Whole Daily

Acknowledgement

My love for baking comes from two incredibly talented and generous women – my Mother and my Gran. Thankyou both for teaching me that patience, a little bit of science but more importantly a whole lot of love are the secret ingredients to successful baking. More importantly though I dedicate this book to my Mum for her selfless dedication to others. Mum, you have always given the best biscuits to the neighbours, and eaten off the chipped plate so that we could have the 'good' ones. I dedicate this book to you because you have given me the greatest gift of all – the desire to help others in order to grow more love in this world.

Thank you.

THE
HAPPY
·PARENT·
PROJECT

Whole foods. Natural healing. Happy thoughts.

Contents.

8   What is Sugar Free Baking?
9   My sugar free baking rules
17   Some tips for baking sugar free
18   Breakfasts
35   Snacks
59   Desserts
82   Glossary of terms
85   Resources
86   Thank you
87   About the author

What is Sugar Free Baking?

SFB can mean lots of different things for different people. It's a confusing world – here's some of the current differing opinions:

- *Diabetics can eat fruit sugars with no worries*
- *Diabetics shouldn't eat honey or fruit – rice malt syrup is the best*
- *Rice malt syrup has arsenic in it – only eat glucose powder*
- *Glucose powder causes stomach aches – stay off ALL sugars!*

Confused? Yup I was too! (don't worry – so are the experts!). Here's one thing everyone seems to agree upon though –refined table sugar is the worst of the lot, it's causing lots of damage to our physical, mental and emotional health – and it's packed into everything! So my opinion is that if we start with kicking that habit, getting it out of our kids diet and increasing the super-foods – well that's a great start and it will make a huge difference to our lives.

So I want to clear up what sugar free baking means for me, and how I've applied it in this book .

Sugar free baking for me is about the following:

- *Finding healthy alternatives to common supermarket cereals*
- *Giving my kids a great start to the day with a nourishing homemade breakfast that isn't pumped with sugar*
- *Baking lovely treats to show my kids how much I love them without feeling that I'm giving them arsenic as I do so*
- *Cleaning up my kids allergies and rashes without having to deprive them of treats*

In this book I've used natural alternatives to white sugar such as honey, rice malt syrup or fruit. You will note that the quantities are small – this is because if you take in any form of sweetener in excess it's going to cause problems in your body.

I have ensured that most recipes have fibre, protein, fats and superfoods blended in – that way you're always giving your kids and yourself a powerpacked snack every time!

My Sugar Free Baking rules

When I teach my sugar free baking classes these are the 3 rules that I want my participants to go home with:

- *Always use an alternative to processed white flour*
- *Always use an alternative to processed white sugar*
- *Add in the good stuff!*

See the tables over the next few pages for the alternatives that you can use.

Flour alternatives

Flour	Pro's	Con's	Flavour	How to use	Buying Tips
Spelt — An ancient variety of wheat with a higher protein, B vitamin, potassium and iron content than wheat	Medium GI (wheat flour is high). Still produces a baked product similar to wheat	Baking doesn't rise as high. Contains gluten (no good if you can't handle wheat)	Mild – similar to wheat flour	As you would wheat flour	Look for Organic and unbleached. Can be found at supermarkets
Buckwheat — Not a grain. Is a plant related to rhubarb but has grain like seeds	Low GI. Good if you can't tolerate wheat. Works fairly well in place of wheat flour in baking. Mild flavor. Easy to make	Doesn't rise as high as flour. Quite expensive	Mild	Follow GF rules (see over page)	Purchase at health food stores

Sugar Free Baking | 9

Flour Alternatives

Flour	Pro's	Con's	Flavour	How to use	Buying Tips
Quinoa — Grain cultivated in South America - known as a superfood	Superfood; Low GI; High in protein & 9 Amino Acids; High in fibre; High in antioxidants	Doesn't rise as high as wheat flour; Expensive	Medium - you can detect a different taste in your baking	Follow GF rules	Purchase at health food stores
Coconut — Ground down coconut flesh	Low GI; High in nutrients	Absorbs a lot of moisture leaving baking dry; Overpowering flavor	Strong	Follow GF rules; Don't use on it's own - mix with another flour	Purchase at health food stores
Almond Meal — Ground down almonds	Low GI; Good source of nutrients and healthy fats; Makes lovely moist/ dense cakes	Baked goods don't rise very high	Mild	Follow GF rules; A very good choice for 'flourless' type recipes that aren't supposed to rise	Make yourself or purchase at health food stores

Rules for baking with gluten free flours

Alternative flours are generally gluten free. Gluten is a protein found in wheat, barley and rye. It gives your baking elasticity, helps it to bind together, to rise and to be soft. When baking Gluten Free you need to:

➡ *Add more of the binding agent (ie increase eggs or add Chia seeds – 1Tb Chia Seeds mixed with 1 Tb water)*

➡ *Use more liquid as other flours absorb more moisture than wheat flour*

➡ *If you need more than 1/4 of a cup of flour in your recipe, use a pre-mixed one or it might not turn out how you want.*

➡ *Once you get used to baking with Gluten Free flours start experimenting with making your own based on your taste preferences.*

sugar alternatives

Sweetener	Pro's	Con's	Flavour	How to use	Buying Tips
Honey Product of nectar from bees	Full of trace minerals. Contains natural antibiotics. Potentially assists in the management of allergies if you buy local	High in fructose	Varied depending on variety – go for a mellow flavor for baking or it will overpower your finished product	Honey is slightly sweeter and denser than sugar so use about 1/4 less honey than if you were using sugar. Reduce liquids by 1/4 cup. Honey burns quicker than sugar	Raw honey is best as it is higher in nutrients. Organic. Local (this helps your body to fight allergies in your local area)
Rice Malt Syrup (Rice that is cultured with enzymes to break down the starches and then cooked till it becomes a syrup)	Low GI. High in nutrients. Nil fructose. Nice flavor. Versatile due to it's mellow flavour	Can be expensive	Mellow	Substitute 1 cup of sugar for 1 1/4 cups of Rice Malt Syrup. Reduce liquids by 1/4 cup	Look for Organic as rice can contain (very low – within food standard guidelines) levels of arsenic
Agave Nectar The juice from the leaves of the agave plant from Mexico/ South America. The juice is heated up into a sugar which is a chemically driven process	Low GI. Sweeter than sugar and honey so you use less.	Very high in fructose	Very sweet and it has a bit of an aftertaste	For every cup of sugar use 2/3 cup of Agave and reduce liquids by 1/4 cup	Do your research first

Sugar Free Baking | 11

sugar alternatives

Sweetener	Pro's	Con's	Flavour	How to use	Buying Tips
Coconut Sugar — The sap collected from the Coconut tree which is then boiled, solidified and made into sugar	Low GI. Comes from sustainable farming methods. Contains some minerals and nutrients	Very high in fructose	Beautiful toffee like flavor. Not too sweet	Substitute cup for cup with normal sugar	
Stevia — Natural sweeteners from the Stevia plant leaves are extracted. They are 300 times stronger than table sugar	Low GI. You only need a small amount due to it's sweetness. No fructose	There are ongoing debates in the wellness world as to the safety of Stevia. It has been approved for use by The Foods Standards Australia New Zealand.	Very sweet	1 cup sugar = 1 tsp stevia	Do your research first
Dates	Come packed with fibre. Very sweet so a good alternative to sugar. Full of vitamins and minerals. Medium GI	Very high in fructose. Will have a laxative effect due to fructose if you eat too many	Sweet	Great for raw foods, smoothies, cheesecake bases etc. Soak for 10 minutes in boiling water before using if dried	Medjool is a superior date in flavor and texture if you can afford it, but if not then buy dried and soak them for 10 minutes.

Sugar Free Baking

sugar alternatives

Sweetener	Pro's	Con's	Flavour	How to use	Buying Tips
Apples	Come packed with fibre, nutrients and minerals Great alternative to sugar in baked cakes and biscuits Great alternative to eggs if you are egg intolerant as they bulk up the baking	Very high in fructose	Sweet	Make into a sauce first by boiling down with a little water then pureeing Use cup for cup as you would sugar Reduce oven temperature as the fruit sugars burn quicker Add more flour to absorb extra liquid	
Bananas	Come packed with fibre, nutrients and minerals Great alternative to sugar in all baked goods almost	Very high in fructose Some people can tolerate bananas well	Sweet	Mash and use cup for cup as you would sugar	The riper the better but this also increases fructose

add in the good stuff!

Now the fun part! Let's add in all the good stuff to our baking and trick our kids and husband's into eating superfoods, veges and healthy fats while they think we're giving them a treat!

Here's my favourite additions (there's heaps more too – you've just got to be brave enough to try them).

the good stuff

Food	Pro's	Con's	Flavour	How to use	Buying Tips
Cacao (Car-Cow) The clean and raw version of Cocoa	Full of antioxidants, magnesium, iron, chromium, zinc, fatty acids and heaps of other good stuff!	If you use too much you can make your baking bitter	Chocolatey without the added sugar or flavourings	Use as you would cocoa. Add to smoothies	From your health food store
Chia Seeds Small seeds that are a complete protein with all 8 essential amino acids	High in fibre. 8 x more Omega 3 than Salmon. High in antioxidants. 5 x more calcium than milk. 3 x more iron than spinach. Great for your skin, hair and nails	Expensive	Nil flavor – they absorb the flavor you add to them	Chia Puddings. Add to bliss balls. Use in place of eggs (1 Tb Chia to 1 Tb water). Put into granola. Add to your biscuits and cakes	

Sugar Free Baking | 14

the good stuff

Food	Pro's	Con's	Flavour	How to use	Buying Tips
Coconut Butter/Oil	Antiviral/antimicrobial/antifungal properties (immune system building) Helps normalize cholesterol levels Stabilises blood sugar Supports digestion Can be heated to a high temperature without going rancid		Like coconut!	Coconut oil is best for cooking and baking with, sometimes you will need to melt it down. Coconut butter includes the flesh of the coconut and can be very dense and difficult to bake with. It can depend on the brand, so play around with a few until you find one that you like	Cold pressed and stored in a dark glass (Loving Earth)
Avocado	High in monounsaturated fat Adding avocado to other foods helps you to absorb their nutrients Protects against liver damage Helps reduce cholesterol	Expensive	Mild	Add to baking, salads, smoothies Make desserts, or eat on it's own	
Tahini and Nut Butters Ground down nuts	Full of vitamins and minerals Lowers cholesterol High in mono-unsaturated fat High in magnesium (stress reducing) Reduces GI of other foods when added			Add to smoothies Have on toast Eat midafternoon to cut sugar cravings Add to bliss balls	Look for no added salt or other nasties – just the nuts ground down

Sugar Free Baking | 15

the good stuff

Food	Pro's	Con's	Flavour	How to use	Buying Tips
Maca — A root from the Andes ground down into a powder	An adaptogen (Balances the hormonal system, nervous system and cardiovascular system); Balances mood; Poweful aphrodisiac; Great for PMS	Expensive. Start slowly when first consuming to let your body get used to it (start with half a teaspoon and build up to 1 Tb)	Mild	Add to smoothies and any baked goods	
Spirulina — An algae – the colour is derived from Chlorophyll. They are the basis of the food chain	The highest concentration of protein in any food; A complete protein source; Anti-inflammatory; As much iron as meat – a powerful blood builder; High in antioxidants; Immune system building		Very powerful! Can take a while to get used to	Add to smoothies, bliss balls; 1 – 2 teaspoons per day adults; 1/2 – 1 teaspoons per day children	Look for an organic brand
Beans	High in antioxidants, fibre, nutrients and minerals; Lower GI of other foods; Keep you fuller for longer	Can be hard to digest causing bloating and gas. To avoid this soak them well and boil them well. Start eating beans slowly – your body learns how to digest beans over time and the gas goes away	Mild	Add to some cakes, muffins	Organic black beans are my favourite

Sugar Free Baking

Some tips for baking sugar free

Sugar Free Baking is a little different to baking with white sugar. Here's a few handy hints:

- *Honey is denser than white sugar therefore when substituting use slightly less honey than you would sugar*

- *Honey causes earlier browning so reduce the cooking time slightly*

- *Sugar binds better than sweeteners which is why some of my recipes call for Chia Seeds – they help to glue things together with the added benefit of being a superfood!*

- *Going 'cold turkey' on sugar is very difficult. Sugar is addictive, especially with children. Try slowly adding the recipes in this book into your baking week and see if your family likes them. Don't take away all of their current favourites, just offer these as well. Take it slowly, have fun with it and don't be discouraged if they don't like it the first time. Change takes time but what a great change it is!*

Breakfasts.

21	Breakfast Smoothies
23	Banana & Coconut Oaty Pancakes
25	Almond Cranberry Granola
27	Coconut Yoghurt
29	Homemade Yoghurt
31	Superfood Bircher Muesli
33	Chocolate Jelly

THE HAPPY PARENT PROJECT

Whole foods. Natural healing. Happy thoughts.

One cannot think well, love well, sleep well, if one has not dined well.

VIRGINIA WOOLF

Breakfast

I know that you know you should be eating breakfast every morning. I also know that if you didn't have 3 loads of washing, school drop off and the groceries to do that you would have breakfast every morning. You have plans that when the kids are at highschool you'll start having breakfast every morning right? But beautiful Mama that's 10 years away! Here's how you're going to start fitting in time for breakfast:

- *Before making a cup of coffee, make your breakfast*
- *Do not turn on the TV until you've had breakfast*
- *Avoid emails, facebook, instagram, twitter, phone messages until you've eaten breakfast*
- *Make everybody's breakfast the night before, set the table and sit down together to eat when you wake up in the morning*
- *If you go for a morning walk, make a smoothie the night before, put it in a bottle in the fridge and take it with you on your walk*
- *If you have a morning commute, do the same as the step above*

It's all about changing habits so I ask you to commit to one of the above for just 5 days. See if you can make it a new habit because honestly it's going to be life changing!

Breakfast is one of the greatest gifts you can give to your growing children. Ditch the sugary cereals, and nourish your children's brains instead with smoothies, granola or chia pudding – they take as long to make as a piece of toast does to cook! Our kids spend the day running, learning, interacting and dealing with emotions so we need to give them the best opportunities to do well in these tasks.

Pancakes - pg 23

Sugar Free Baking | 19

Breakfast Smoothies

Breakfast Smoothies

Perky Nana

2 tsp cacao powder
1/2 teaspoon honey
1 banana (chopped and frozen)
3/4 cup milk of your choice
1/4 cup rolled oats (or flaked quinoa if gluten free)

- Blend together

Strawberry Shortcake

1 cup strawberries, frozen
1/2 banana (chopped and frozen)
1/2 teaspoon honey
1/4 cup rolled oats
3/4 cup milk of your choice

- Blend together

Kiwi Kids

2 kiwifruit
1 banana (chopped and frozen)
3/4 cup milk of your choice
1 tsp honey
1/4 cup rolled oats

- Blend together

Sugar Free Baking | 21

Banana & Coconut Oaty Pancakes

Banana & Coconut Oaty Pancakes

INGREDIENTS

3/4 cup rolled oats
(or quinoa flakes if gluten free)

3/4 cup rice milk

1 egg

1/2 tsp salt

2 Tb honey

3/4 cup (self raising gluten free) flour

2 Tb coconut butter/oil

2 ripe bananas

METHOD

1. Heat coconut butter in a cast iron or heavy pan on the stovetop

2. Mash bananas in a large bowl

3. Add oats, milk, egg and honey to bananas and stir to combine

4. Stir coconut butter into wet ingredients

5. Add dry ingredients and stir gently

6. Drop about 1/2 cup of mixture at a time into pan. When bubbles appear then break on the surface, turn and cook on the other side

7. Serve drizzled with honey or with coconut yoghurt.

Almond Cranberry Granola

Almond Cranberry Granola

INGREDIENTS

1/2 cup honey

1/2 cup coconut butter or your choice of oil

1 tsp vanilla essence

1 tsp ground ginger

1/2 tsp salt

4 cups rolled oats

1 cup shredded coconut

1/2 cup almonds, crushed

1/2 cup sunflower seeds

1/2 cup pumpkin seeds

1/2 cup cranberries, dried

METHOD

1. Pre-heat oven to 150°C

2. Heat first 5 ingredients in saucepan until honey is dissolved

3. In a large baking tray mix together oats, coconut and seeds. Pour honey mixture over the top and stir well until honey is spread through

4. Bake at 150°C for about 15-20 minutes. You will need to watch it carefully and stir every 5 minutes

5. Leave to cool in tray and stir a couple of times during cooling, otherwise it will clump together, then add in the cranberries

6. Store in an airtight container and serve with yoghurt. This is a great afternoon snack for hungry children!

Coconut Yoghurt

Coconut Yoghurt

INGREDIENTS

1 1/2 cans of organic coconut cream (not the light stuff)

1 Tb honey

2 Tb thickener
(I use agar agar - you can use gelatine, arrowroot or tapioca starch if preferred)

1 cup live yoghurt culture (either use 1 cup of yoghurt or 2 probiotic capsules

METHOD

1. In a saucepan heat 1 can of coconut cream, the honey and thickener gently for 5 minutes. Allow to cool to room temperature

2. Add the rest of the ingredients and mix well (so the culture is thoroughly distributed)

3. Pour into your yoghurt container and place in the yoghurt maker as per manufacturers instructions

4. Allow to culture for 12 hours (it requires longer than dairy yoghurt) then refrigerate for 12 hours.

Yoghurt is a childhood favourite, but unfortunately commercial yoghurt is so full of additives, preservatives and flavourings these days that it is no longer the nutritious snack it used to be. Making your own yoghurt at home is easy and cost effective and you can control how sweet it is. Coconut yoghurt is a great alternative for those in the family that are dairy intolerant.

Homemade Yoghurt

Homemade Yoghurt

INGREDIENTS

1 packet of Easiyo Greek yoghurt

1 litre water

1 Tb raw sugar or honey

METHOD

1. Simply follow the instructions on the packet mix, pop the yoghurt into the thermos and wait overnight - in the morning you have thick, creamy healthy yoghurt!

This recipe is made using a yoghurt maker. These can be purchased from most supermarkets or online and have yoghurt mixes which you purchase with them. I have included this method of making yoghurt because it is the easiest and simplest way if you're getting started. Be careful when you buy the packet mixes though – some of them are again loaded with added sugar -purchase the natural Greek yoghurt type. Make up a batch before you go to bed - follow the instructions on the packet and in the morning you'll have fresh, probiotic yoghurt. Learning the art of yoghurt making will seriously reduce your food bill and your children's sugar intake.

Superfood Bircher Muesli

Superfood Bircher Muesli

INGREDIENTS

1/2 cup flaked quinoa

1/2 cup rolled oats

2 Tb chia seeds

2 Tb sunflower seeds

2 Tb goji berries

1 1/2 cups of milk of your choice

1 grated apple

1 Tb honey

1 Tb crushed almonds

Fresh fruit

METHOD

1. Combine the first 6 ingredients in a bowl and cover

2. Leave in the fridge overnight

3. In the morning add the rest of the ingredients

4. Enjoy!

Chia seeds are a powerhouse of nutrients. Adding them to your breakfast each day will keep you fuller for longer and give you sustained energy. They are one of nature's 'superfoods' with omega and amino acids. They form a nice 'gel' when combined with a liquid so you can use them in baking as an egg replacement.

Chocolate Jelly

Chocolate Jelly

INGREDIENTS

2 Tb chia seeds

3/4 cup milk of your choice

1/2 tsp runny honey

1 tsp cacao powder

1 tsp dark organic chocolate shaved or broken up, or cacao nibs

METHOD

1. Mix everything together in a jar or glass and wait about 10 minutes for the chia seeds to set jelly like.

This is definitely one to get the kids involved in making! This can be eaten for breakfast, lunch, as a snack or dessert. It's healthier with loads of antioxidants, omega 3 and just a touch of honey to sweeten. Mum's - this is a great snack for you to eat on the go at 3pm to keep you going too. I top mine with ground almonds, goji berries and some nuts and it keeps me going till dinner.

When a woman bakes she is sculpting her feelings for another into a light, sweet and fluffy edible piece of love. Do not criticize her baking, for when you do, you are not questioning her skill, but the depth of her love for you!

NICOLE BEARDSLEY

Snacks.

39　Gooey On The Inside Crispy On The Outside Chocolate Brownies

41　Chocolate Crackles

43　The Most Awesomest Choc Chip Cookie Ever!

45　Strawberry Ripple Bliss Balls with Sweet Pistachio Sherbert

47　Red Velvet Cup Cakes

49　Icy-Poles

51　Banana Chocolate Muffins

53　After Dinner Mint Truffles

55　Honey Nut Popcorn

57　Hummingbird Cake

Snacks

Making snacks for our kids has to be one of the greatest causes of angst for all mothers! Below are my tips for transitioning your kids over to healthy snacks.

ALWAYS BE PREPARED

You have to think in advance when it comes to snacks. I use a meal planning template (downloadable off my website under resources) to ensure that I have all of the snacks and meals planned out for my week in advance, and so I know that I have the ingredients too. Then I choose one day of the week to prepare all of my snacks so that I can easily just grab something out when the kids or I are hungry.

ADD IN THE GOOD STUFF, DON'T TAKE AWAY THE BAD STUFF (YET)

Most of the time when we make a change for our family's health we become the fun police. All of the stuff that they love and look forward to is suddenly gone, and instead replaced with something that tastes and looks like crap. Here's a different approach – let them have the treats they love – just add good stuff into them. Over time their tastebuds will adjust, they'll get used to new textures and they'll stop associating healthy foods with tasting bad.

Once you're at that point you amp up the good stuff, and slowly decrease the bad stuff (Sugar, flour, colours, additives and preservatives). It's much more sustainable and fun for all involved!

TAKE IT SLOWLY

Think of this as a marathon rather than a sprint. Life is a long time, and you've got heaps and heaps of time to make this transition. Just pick one change per week and keep going with that one until it is well and truly a part of day to day life. Then pick your next change. This way you won't overwhelm yourself and your family with changes – they won't even notice it! For example, you might choose to introduce Oat or Rice milk into your family so that less dairy is being consumed. This might take a month – that's ok. Any change is a change for the better.

BE POSITIVE

Here's something you already know – your kids don't want to change their eating habits – in fact, your husband probably doesn't want to either! The best approach you can take is to focus on the positives rather than the negatives – use reverse psychology on them.

Snacks

If they say 'I'm not drinking a smoothie with spinach in it!" You say "Ok honey, no worries". You're such a good boy for drinking the yummy Oat Milk". I guarantee you that if you keep focusing on the positives and don't make them eat something they don't want too, they'll come around eventually. It's taken me 1 year to get my son to drink a smoothie that is green, but you know what – eventually he did – because it was his choice! I just kept asking him every day if he wanted some of Mummy's green smoothie and every day for a year he said no. But one day he said yes!

ROLE MODELLING

As above – your kids (and hubby) have never thought about a different way of eating – they're quite happy and content where they are. The best approach is just to start doing it yourself – don't put pressure on them to do it with you, just let them watch and observe what you're doing. They'll ask questions – you'll answer them. They'll have a taste every now and then, and eventually they'll give it a go themselves – and realize it's not that bad!

EDUCATION

Kids need to know why – husbands do too. You need to be able to explain why you're introducing a new food and how it's going to help them. So do your research. My husband's favourite beer was one that was full of preservatives. I explained to him the side effects of preservatives (headaches, mood swings) and suggested he might like to try a boutique beer instead. He tried it and was shocked that he woke up in the morning feeling no hangover. I kept reinforcing each time he had preservative free beer that he seemed better in the mornings. He is now the biggest advocate for boutique beers out there!

EXPECT RELAPSES

Don't expect to succeed straight away. Your kids are going to often crave sugary, colorful foods – marketing and media is very powerful. You will do your best job and they will still choose to have a Coke at a school sausage sizzle – you can't control that. But you are doing a wonderful, wonderful job of implanting the seed of healthy eating in their brain. And one day, they're going to surprise you – they're going to make a healthy choice at a birthday party, or they're going to drink some of your green smoothie and say 'Yum' and you are going to be so, so, so proud and it will all be worth it. I promise you!

Gooey On The Inside Crispy On The Outside Chocolate Brownies

Gooey On The Inside Crispy On The Outside Chocolate Brownies

INGREDIENTS

2 cans black beans

4 Tb cacao

1 cup flaked quinoa

1/4 cup ground buckwheat groats or buckwheat flour

1/2 tsp salt

6 Tb honey

1/2 cup coconut butter

4 tsp vanilla extract

1 tsp baking powder

1/2 cup sugar free dark chocolate (at least 75% cocoa minimum) broken up – I use Luvju

METHOD

1. Preheat oven to 160°C

2. Grease an 8x8 pan. Combine all ingredients except chocolate in a food processor and blend until completely smooth

3. Stir in the chocolate. Pour into pan and sprinkle with extra chocolate if you want

4. Cook for about 45 minutes then let cool for at least 1 hour in the pan (I actually put mine into the fridge for a little while to help it to set before cutting it up).

Chocolate Crackles

Chocolate Crackles

INGREDIENTS

4 cups brown rice puffs (or rice bubbles but check first to ensure there are no hidden sugars)

2 Tb honey

2 Tb cacao

1 cup coconut butter

METHOD

1. Put rice puffs into a large bowl
2. Melt all other ingredients in a saucepan until combined
3. Mix into rice puff mixture and stir well
4. Spoon into muffin cases
5. Refrigerate until firm.

The Most Awesomest Choc Chip Cookie Ever!

The Most Awesomest Choc Chip Cookie Ever!

INGREDIENTS

2 cups almond meal

1/2 tsp baking soda

1/3 cup coconut sugar

1 organic egg

Pinch of salt

1/3 cup coconut oil, melted

1 teaspoon vanilla essence

1/2 cup dark organic chocolate smashed up (you could use Green & Blacks or Luvju)

METHOD

1. Mix the almond, sugar, salt and baking soda together. Mix in the wet ingredients and chocolate. The mixture should be quite wet – that's ok.

2. Roll into balls and place on a greased oven tray

3. Bake at 160°C for 10-15 minutes until golden. It's ok if they're still a little soft when you take them out – they'll harden up as they cool.

Makes 24.

Strawberry Ripple Bliss Balls with Sweet Pistachio Sherbert

Strawberry Ripple Bliss Balls with Sweet Pistachio Sherbert

INGREDIENTS

330 grams raw almonds

1 cup coconut

1 Tb melted coconut butter

1 cup strawberries

1 cup dates (if using dried, soak in boiling water for ten minutes)

1 tsp vanilla essence

2 Tb cacao

1/4 cup sunflower seeds

2 tsp protein powder or Vital Greens (optional)

1/2 cup pistachios

1/2 cup dehydrated strawberries (or goji berries)

METHOD

1. Process almonds until they resemble bread crumbs

2. Add all other ingredients except for pistachios and dehydrated strawberries

3. Blend until the mixture comes together (if too wet add some more sunflower seeds - if too dry add a dash of water)

4. Roll into balls and place on a plate

5. Crush pistachio's and dehydrated strawberries (I use a mortar and pestle)

6. Roll balls in this mixture

7. Place in an airtight container and store in the fridge or freezer (depending on how hard you like them!).

Red Velvet Cup Cakes

Red Velvet Cup Cakes

INGREDIENTS

1 large fresh beetroot (or three small)

175g gluten free flour

2 Tb honey

1 tsp gluten free baking powder

2 Tb cacao or cocoa

2 free range eggs

1/4 cup milk of your choice (cows, rice, soy)

1/4 cup oil of your choice (I use rice bran)

60g coconut butter (or butter if you prefer)

1 cup dates (if dried - soaked for 10 mins in boiling water first)

METHOD

1. Trim edges off beetroot and grate by hand or use attachment on food processor (the easiest option!)
2. Sift dry ingredients together in a bowl
3. Whisk eggs and milk together in a separate bowl
4. Leave beetroot in food processor and add dates, honey, butter (or coconut oil) and oil. Process until smooth and creamy
5. Gradually add milk/egg mixture and process again, then add to dry ingredients
6. Fold together gently
7. Spoon into muffin tins. Optional: break off a small square of organic dark chocolate and push into the centre of each muffin. This really makes them taste amazing!
8. Bake for 15-20 minutes in a pre-heated moderate oven then leave to cool for 5-10 mins before turning out onto a cooling rack.

Icy-Poles

Icy-Poles

INGREDIENTS

Use any of the smoothie recipes in the breakfast section to make your icy-poles.

OTHER FLAVOUR OPTIONS

Apple juice

Green smoothies

Vege juice (with some apple juice added to sweeten)

Water with chunks of fruit to make it look pretty

Kefir water for a pro-biotic icy pole!

METHOD

1. Simply pour the smoothie into your icy pole mold and freeze for 3-4 hours

2. Use warm water to loosen the mold to get the icy pole out.

This is a great way to use up left over smoothies in the morning - it's time saving and money saving and kids LOVE anything that is frozen! I always make extra smoothie in the morning and then make Icy poles for afternoon tea or dessert - it's the easiest meal ever (and keeps the kids quiet for a good 20 minutes!)

Banana Chocolate Muffins

Banana Chocolate Muffins

INGREDIENTS

2 ripe bananas, mashed

2 Tb honey

1 egg

3 Tb coconut butter

1/2 tsp salt

3/4 tsp baking soda

1 cup self raising gluten free flour

1/2 cup flaked quinoa

1/2 cup dark organic chocolate

1/4 cup milk of your choice

METHOD

1. Pre-heat oven to 180°C
2. Grease muffin tins
3. Mix together banana, honey, egg, milk and coconut butter
4. Break chocolate into pieces
5. Add dry ingredients and chocolate to wet ingredients and mix gently
6. Spoon into muffin tins
7. Bake for 10-15 mins or until muffins spring back to the touch
8. Cool for 10 minutes before removing from pan.

nom nom nom!

After Dinner Mint Truffles

After Dinner Mint Truffles

INGREDIENTS

200 grams raw almonds

1 1/2 cups dates

2 Tb coconut oil

2 Tb honey

1 tsp vanilla

1/2 cup sunflower seeds

3 Tb cacao

1 Tb tahini or nut butter

1/4 tsp salt

1 cup shredded coconut

4-5 drops peppermint essence

METHOD

1. Using a food processor, process almonds until they resemble breadcrumbs

2. Add the dates and process for 1 minute

3. Add all other ingredients

4. Roll into balls

5. Place in a container with a lid and store in the freezer

6. Roll in cacao if you wish.

Honey Nut Popcorn

Honey Nut Popcorn

INGREDIENTS

2 Tb oil

1/2 cup corn kernels

1/2 cup crushed almonds

1/3 cup honey

1tsp vanilla essence

1 Tb lemon juice

1 Tb coconut cream

3 Tb water

Pinch salt

METHOD

1. In a saucepan with a lid heat 2 Tb oil
2. Pour in the Corn Kernels and swirl in the oil to coat
3. Put the lid on and make sure the heat is medium
4. Once the Corn starts popping turn the heat down to low
5. Once 3/4 of the Corn is popped, turn the heat off so that the rest don't burn. They'll continue to pop on their own
6. Turn the oven onto 150°C and oil 2 baking trays
7. In a saucepan mix the honey, vanilla, lemon, coconut cream, water and salt
8. Stir frequently for 5-8 minutes until the sauce thickens. Add the corn and nuts to sauce and mix to coat. Put onto a baking tray in a single layer
9. Bake for 10-15 minutes, turning once
10. Leave to cool then enjoy!

Hummingbird Cake

Hummingbird Cake

INGREDIENTS

1 cup dates (soaked in boiling water for 10 mins if dried)

250grams gluten free self-raising flour

2 bananas mashed

1x 440g can of crushed pineapple, drained

1/2 tsp cinnamon

1/2 cup shredded coconut

1 cup rice bran oil (or your oil of choice)

1/2 cup chopped walnuts

1/2 cup rice malt syrup (or honey)

2 Tb chia seeds (soaked in 1 Tb water) – or use 2 eggs if you prefer

METHOD

1. Pre-heat oven to 180°C

2. Drain the water from the dates, then add the chia seeds, rice malt syrup and oil and food process all together

3. Add this mixture to all of the other ingredients and stir gently

4. Pour into a round cake pan that has been oiled and lined with baking paper

5. Bake for 30-45 minutes until a skewer inserted into the centre comes out clean

6. Leave in the pan for 10 minutes, then turn out onto a cooling rack.

You can ice this with cream-cheese frosting (which obviously has dairy and sugar in it) or if you want to keep it super healthy then serve it with a spoonful of coconut yoghurt.

The only real stumbling block is fear of failure. In cooking you've got to have a what-the-hell attitude.

JULIA CHILD

Desserts.

61 Apple and Pineapple Jelly

63 Fruit Salad with Rosewater and Mint

65 Raw Berry Cheesecake

67 Chocolate Mousse

69 Blueberry Ice-cream

71 Mint Chocolate Chip Ice-Cream

73 Banana Chocolate Ice-Cream

75 Power Packed Apple Crumble

77 Black Forest Mousse

79 Chocolate Toffee Cups

81 Blow Your Mind Banoffee Bowl

Apple and Pineapple Jelly

Apple and Pineapple Jelly

INGREDIENTS

2 cups organic apple juice

1 tsp agar agar (or *gelatine)

1/2 cup crushed pineapple, drained

METHOD

1. Pour the juice into a pot and add the agar agar or gelatine

2. Heat slowly for 5 minutes then leave to cool

3. Once cool add the pineapple

4. Pour into a bowl, cover and leave in the fridge to set

5. If you want to make it into a pretty shape like in the photo, wait until it has set then give it a stir and spoon into cookie cutter moulds on a plate. Squash it down and put back in the fridge for 5-10 minutes.

*see glossary of terms

Fruit Salad with Rosewater and Mint

Fruit Salad with Rosewater and Mint

INGREDIENTS

1/4 of a watermelon

1/4 of a rockmelon

1 cup of strawberries

Handful of blueberries

3 tsp rosewater

Handful of mint

1 tsp honey

METHOD

1. Using a melon baller* make balls out of the watermelon and rockmelon. Put all fruit into a serving bowl

2. In a pot, dissolve honey in 1/2 a cup of water over a low heat. Add the rosewater then turn off heat and leave to cool

3. Pour over the fruit and mix gently. Decorate with mint leaves.

4. Store in the fridge until ready to eat.

* Melon ballers are available at any Chefs Essential shop for about $3. They're worth the small investment for this salad as it is so eye catching and the perfect dinner party dessert - kids love the novelty of the fruit balls too!

Raw Berry Cheesecake

Raw Berry Cheesecake

INGREDIENTS

BASE:

1/2 cup raw almonds

1 cup shredded coconut

1 Tb honey

2 1/2 Tb coconut oil

1/2 tsp vanilla essence

Pinch salt

Handful dates

FILLING:

2 cups cashews

2 cups blueberries

1/2 cup coconut oil

1/2 cup lemon juice

1 tsp vanilla essence

1/4 cup water

METHOD

1. Soak the almonds and cashews for 4 hours or overnight (in separate bowls)

2. Soak the dates (if using dried) in boiling water for 10 minutes

3. Process the base ingredients until they resemble bread crumbs or start coming together

4. Press into a greased pie dish or cheesecake pan

5. Process the filling ingredients until smooth

6. Pour over the base and smooth the top

7. Freeze until ready to serve (at least 3 hours)

8. Before serving, sit at room temperature for 10 minutes to soften

9. Garnish with extra coconut and blueberries.

Chocolate Mousse

Chocolate Mousse

INGREDIENTS

1 ripe avocado

1 Tb honey

1/4 tsp salt

Handful of dates (soaked in boiling water for 10 mins if using dried)

3 Tb cacao powder

METHOD

1. Place all ingredients in a bowl

2. Using a stick blender (or food processor) blend until smooth

3. Place in the fridge until chilled

4. To make a shape - oil a cookie cutter and place on a plate. Fill with mousse mixture. Remove cookie cutter gently, alternatively, just place in a glass or jar

5. Top with fresh dates.

Blueberry Ice-Cream

Blueberry Ice Cream

INGREDIENTS

2 cans coconut cream

2 cups blueberries (or your choice of berries)

2 Tb honey

1 cup dates (soaked for 10 minutes if using dried)

METHOD

1. Place all ingredients in a blender (if using frozen blueberries add these last or they will freeze the honey and it won't blend)
2. Pour into a plastic container
3. Freeze for 1 hour
4. Stir
5. Freeze again
6. Before serving, sit at room temperature for 15 minutes (or microwave if you have one).*

* There is a growing concern that many commercial ice-creams contain ingredients to keep their ice-cream soft that you don't necessarily want to be feeding your children. Home made ice-cream therefore has that annoying problem that it's rock hard when you take it out of the freezer. It's just one of those things you have to deal with when you move to clean eating, so get into the practice of taking it out of the freezer when you serve up dinner so it's nice and soft by dessert time!

Sugar Free Baking | 69

Mint Chocolate Chip Ice-Cream

Mint Chocolate Chip Ice-Cream

INGREDIENTS

2 cans coconut cream

4 drops peppermint essence

1/4 cup dark organic chocolate

2 Tb honey

1 tsp vanilla essence

METHOD

1. Blend everything in a blender except chocolate until smooth

2. Break up chocolate into small bits

3. Stir chocolate through the icecream with a spoon

4. Pour into a plastic container

5. Freeze for 1 hour

6. Stir

7. Freeze again

8. Before serving, sit at room temperature for 15 minutes (or microwave if you have one).

Banana Chocolate Chip Ice-Cream

Banana Chocolate Chip Ice-Cream

INGREDIENTS

2 ripe bananas (chopped up and frozen)

1 can coconut cream (or your choice of milk)

2 Tb cacao powder

1 cup dates (soaked for 10 minutes if using dried)

METHOD

1. Blend the coconut cream, honey and dates until smooth

2. Add all other ingredients and blend

3. Pour into a plastic container

4. Freeze for 1 hour

5. Stir

6. Freeze again

7. Before serving, sit at room temperature for 15 minutes (or microwave if you have one).

Handy Hint: Buy up cheap ripe bananas that no-body else wants and cut them up and store them in your freezer for smoothies and icecream.

Power Packed Apple Crumble

Power Packed Apple Crumble

INGREDIENTS

1/2 cup rolled oats

1/2 cup gluten free flour

1 cup chopped walnuts

2 Tb chia seeds

1 Tb ground flaxseeds

1/2 cup flaked quinoa

1-2 Tb honey

100gms coconut butter (or normal butter if not dairy intolerant)

2 cups stewed apples

METHOD

1. Pre-heat oven to 180°C
2. Grease a pudding dish
3. Pour the apples into the base of the dish
4. Melt coconut butter and honey together in a saucepan
5. Mix together rolled oats, flour, walnuts, chia seeds, flaxseeds and quinoa
6. Pour the honey mixture into the dry ingredients and mix well
7. Crumble the mixture over the top of the apples
8. Bake until crumble is golden and crispy on top
9. Serve with ice-cream.

Black Forest Mousse

Black Forest Mousse

INGREDIENTS

FOR THE MOUSSE:

1 ripe avocado

2 tsp cacao

1 cup dates (soaked for 10 minutes if using dried)

1/2 tsp salt

2 tsp honey

FOR THE BERRY SAUCE:

1/2 cup fresh or frozen berries

1/4 cup chia seeds

2 tsp honey

2 Tb water

FOR THE CREAM:

Coconut cream (sit in the fridge for half an hour or so first)

METHOD

1. For the Mousse, blend everything together until smooth

2. For the Berry Sauce, boil everything together on the stove for about 5 minutes. If the berries haven't broken down then give them a bit of a mash with a fork. Leave to cool

3. Now grab yourself a glass and start layering! Place some of the Mousse in the bottom of the glass, top with a tablespoon of coconut cream and then some sauce. Repeat this a couple of times so it looks pretty. Sprinkle with some nuts or shredded coconut then let sit in the fridge for 10 minutes or so until it's cold. Enjoy!

Chocolate Toffee Cups

Chocolate Toffee Cups

INGREDIENTS

FOR THE CHOCOLATE:

1/2 cup coconut butter

1/2 cup cacao

Pinch of salt

2 Tb rice malt syrup (or honey if you prefer)

FOR THE BANOFFEE SAUCE:

1/4 cup tahini

1 mashed banana

1/4 cup honey

1 tsp vanilla

METHOD

1. Melt the chocolate ingredients together in a saucepan. Stir well
2. Line some muffin trays (the small kiddie sized one's are the best) with patty/muffin cases
3. Pour in a teaspoon of the sauce into the bottom of each case
4. Place in the freezer for 10 minutes
5. Whilst these are freezing, mix all of the sauce ingredients together using a stick blender
6. Bring the pan out of the freezer and place half a teaspoon of the banoffee sauce in the middle of each chocolate
7. Place back in the freezer for 5 minutes
8. Bring out and pour another teaspoon of chocolate over the top (to cover the banoffie sauce)
9. Place back in the freezer until set
10. Once set, store in an airtight container in the freezer.

Blow Your Mind Banoffee Bowl

Blow Your Mind Banoffee Bowl

INGREDIENTS

FOR THE CHIA PUDDING:

3 Tb Chia Seeds

1 Cup Oat Milk (or milk of your choice)

2 tsp Honey

2 tsp Vanilla

FOR THE BANOFFEE SAUCE:

1/2 Cup Tahini (or nut butter)

2 mashed Bananas

1/4 cup honey

2 tsp Vanilla

FOR THE CHOCOLATE SAUCE

1/4 cup dark sugar free chocolate

METHOD

1. In a bowl mix together all of the chia pudding ingredients and allow to sit for 20 minutes

2. In the meantime, mix together all of the sauce ingredients and then use a stick blender to blend until smooth

3. Using the double boiler method, melt the chocolate

4. Now it's time to layer!

5. Place 2 Tb of the pudding in the bottom of a glass (makes enough for about 2 standard glasses)

6. Top with 2 Tb of the sauce

7. Repeat

8. Pour 1 Tb of the chocolate over the top

9. Decorate with sliced bananas.

Glossary of terms

When I first started buying wholefoods and baking with them I had no idea how to pronounce them or how to use them. I remember googling 'How to pronounce Quinoa' just so that I wouldn't look like an idiot next time I went to the Organic shop! This glossary is here to help you to understand what these super crazy foods are, how to pronounce them and how to use them!

AGAR AGAR

This is a seaweed derived 'gelatine' and is what is used in the petri dishes in science class! I use it because it is preservative free, unlike many supermarket gelatine's. Many supermarket gelatine's are derived from animals and requires preservative 220 (A big 'no no' if you have asthma or allergies in your family).

CHIA SEEDS ('CHEE -AH')

These are small seeds which are a power house of nutrients and very high in Omega 3 fatty acids. Chia seeds are reasonably high in fat (9 grams per 28 gram serving). When added to water they form a gel and can be used as an egg replacement.

COCONUT BUTTER/ OIL

This is a great alternative to butter or oil. It has a high burning point which means it's a better alternative for frying as it doesn't become carcinogenic like other oils. At room temperature the oil can be whipped and creamed like normal butter. When melted it can be used like a regular oil.

CACAO ('CAR-COW')

Cacao is the powder that is derived from the Cocoa Beans. It is the raw unrefined version, as opposed to Cocoa. Cocoa often has flavourings added to it as well. Cacao is high in magnesium which is great for stress relief.

COCONUT CREAM/MILK

This is a great dairy alternative to standard cream. It comes from the flesh of the coconut. Can be used to make icecream, added to smoothies, in curries etc.

Glossary of terms

FLAXSEEDS

Flaxseeds are a really valuable fibre source and high in Omega 3 fatty acids. They need to be ground in order to be digested so make sure you buy the ground version. They also need to be refrigerated once opened. You can find them at most supermarkets or wholefood shops.

RICE MILK

A great dairy alternative. It comes in box form at the super market. Make sure you buy unsweetened as Rice Milk already has a natural sweetness. Kids love it!

QUINOA ('KEEN - WAH')

An ancient grain from South America that can be used in place of rice for salads, sushi or with a hot meal. Comes in red, black and white. Also comes 'flaked' which is great for puddings. It's rich in protein, high in fibre, gluten free and low GI.

ROSEWATER

This is water that is the byproduct of the production of Rose Oil. It is flavoured with and smells of Roses and is beautiful added to pastries or fruit salads. You will find this at most high quality delicatessens.

Resources.

Resources

If you found this book helpful and want to know more about transitioning your family to a healthier lifestyle:

VISIT MY BLOG:

thehappyparentproject.com for free tips, tricks and recipes

FIND ME ON FACEBOOK:

https://www.facebook.com/thehappyparentproject

FIND INSPIRATION ON INSTAGRAM:

http://instagram.com/thehappyparentproject

CHECK ME OUT ON PINTEREST:

http://www.pinterest.com/happyparent1

Remember to upload photos of your sugar free creations to the sites and #THPP and #SFB on instagram!

Thank You

To the wonderful Mama's that connect with me each day in person and on social media and constantly motivate me to continue doing the work I love.

To Luke, Jesse, Andi and Josh - my beautiful family for being my support crew on the long road I've travelled to put this book to print

To Lauren Glucina for turning my recipes into works of art. I will be eternally grateful for the love and passion that you put into taking this caterpillar of a book and turning it into a butterfly!

xox

About The Author

Nicole Beardsley is a Mother, Wife, Occupational Therapist, Health Coach, Blogger and Author. Her work is supporting busy Mum's to take those first steps to transition their family to a healthier lifestyle.

Nicole's passion for helping other busy Mum's has come from 14 years of having an absolute blast with her kids and learning the winning formula for being a happy parent. She and her family have lived on four corners of the globe, connecting with remote cultures, sometimes living on the bare minimums but always having a great time. She says that it's not a scientific formula but simply whole foods, natural healing and happy thoughts that win through in the end, for any culture.

She is now taking her knowledge to mum's all over the world to inspire and motivate them to be happy parents.

Notes

Orange, Almond + choc muffins

40 g butter.

½ cup honey

1 Egg

120g plain flour